HANNAH
goes to
The Dentist

by Helen and Clive Dorman

Paediatric Consultant:
Dr Huw R Jenkins MA MD FRCP FRCPCH

CP Publishing

Let us say hello to Hannah and the people she meets at the dentist.

Hello Hannah.

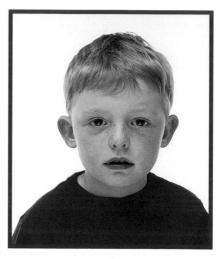

Hello Anthony.

Hello Kathy and Jessica. Kathy is Anthony's and Jessica's mummy.

Hello Jackie. Jackie is the receptionist.

Hello Marie. Marie
is the dental nurse.

Hello Katrina.
Katrina is the dentist.

We visit the dentist to make sure our teeth are healthy.
Let us turn the pages and find out what Hannah is going
to do at the dentist today.

Hannah is arriving at the dentist with her mummy. Hannah has been to the dentist before but she cannot remember what happens, so she is feeling a little shy.

Do you feel shy sometimes?
When do you feel shy?

Jackie is the receptionist. A receptionist answers the phone and makes appointments for the dentist. Hannah's mummy is telling Jackie that Hannah has arrived.

Hannah is playing with the toys in the waiting room. The waiting room is where we wait for our turn to see the dentist.

1 Hannah's friend Anthony has arrived.
   Anthony is also seeing the dentist today.

2 Jessica, Anthony's sister, is sitting with
   their mummy, Kathy.

3 Kathy is showing Hannah's mummy Jessica's new teeth.
Even though Jessica is only small she is also going to see the dentist.
She has been visiting the dentist with her mummy since she was born.

How many of Jessica's teeth can you count?

Marie has called out Hannah's name, it is her turn to see the dentist.

Marie holds Hannah's hand. She is going to show her where to go next.

Marie is a dental nurse. She helps the dentist.

Do you know where other nurses work?

Can you name the foods?

Marie has a baby in her tummy.
Even in Marie's tummy her baby has teeth that are
growing. They are growing in the gums.
These teeth are called 'buds'.
If Marie eats the right foods, her teeth will stay strong
and her baby's teeth will grow strong, too.
Some of the foods and drinks she needs are shown below.

Can you name the foods and drinks in the picture?

1 Hannah is shy when she meets Katrina. Katrina is the dentist and Hannah has forgotten what she looked liked.

2 Katrina suggests mummy sits on the dentist's chair with Hannah. Hannah needs a reassuring hug.

Katrina puts on a new pair of rubber gloves. She puts
on clean rubber gloves for each patient to keep her
hands hygienic.
Mouths have a lot of germs. Katrina will put her
fingers in a lot of different people's mouths today.

Where else do we find germs?
When do people wear rubber gloves?

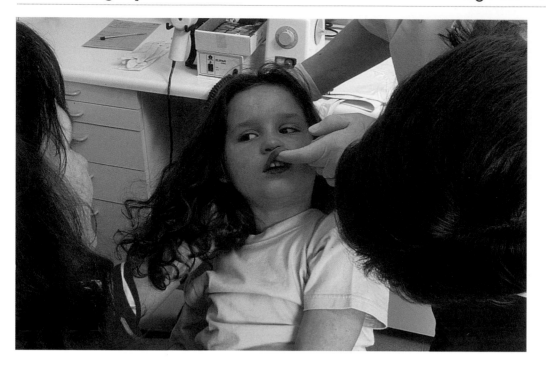

1 Katrina gently lifts Hannah's lip to look at her top teeth. At first, Hannah is not sure if she likes this.

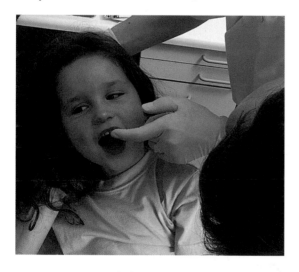

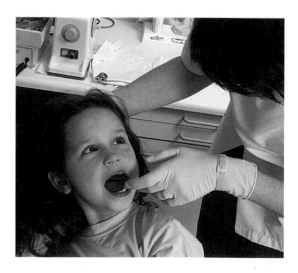

2 Reassured by mummy, Hannah feels better and opens her mouth.

3 Katrina can now look at all Hannah's teeth.

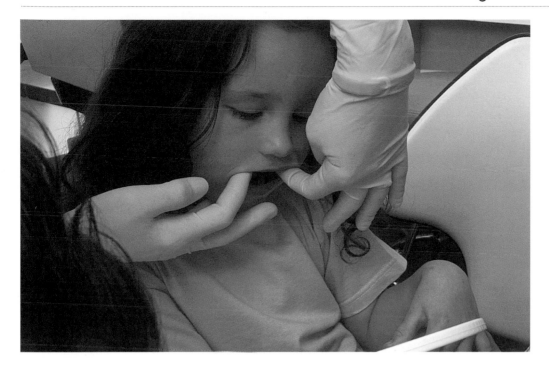

4 Katrina gets a mirror so that Hannah can see and count her teeth.

5 Hannah counts her teeth.

How many teeth have you got?

1 Hannah is now sitting in Katrina's dentist's chair.

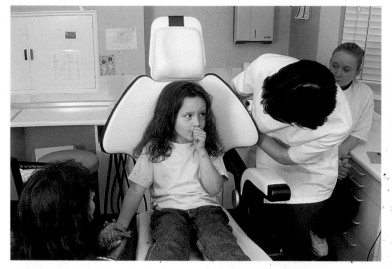

2 Katrina shows Hannah that her magic chair can go back...

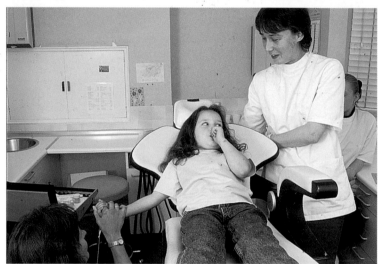

3 ... and up! Hannah thinks it is good fun.

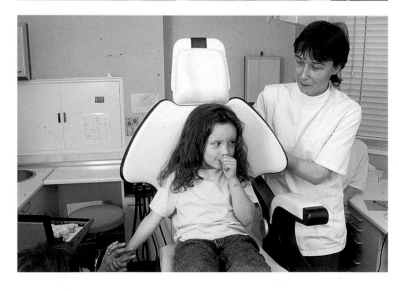

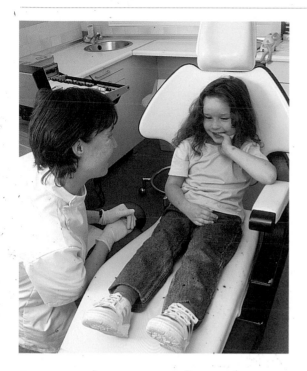

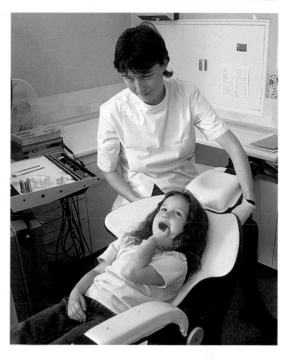

4 Hannah is now happy on the chair.

5 Katrina lowers the back of the chair.

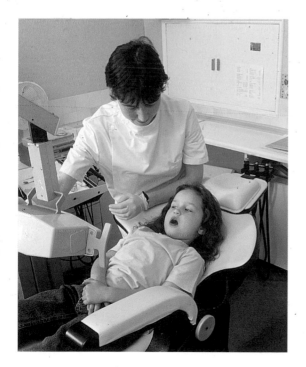

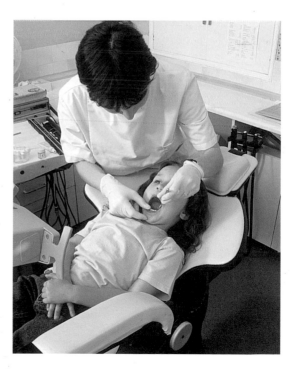

6 She shines a bright light into Hannah's mouth.

7 Katrina now begins to check Hannah's teeth.

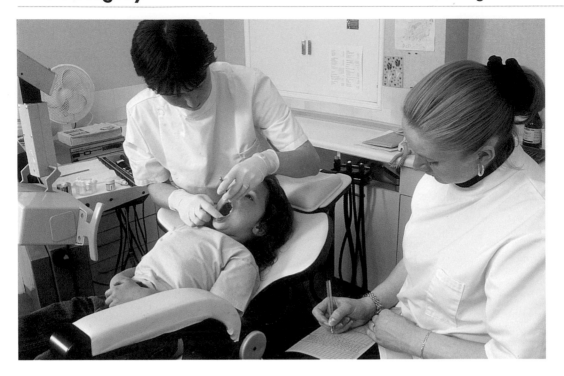

1 Katrina uses a silver tool with a mirror to look behind Hannah's teeth. Marie is ready to make notes.

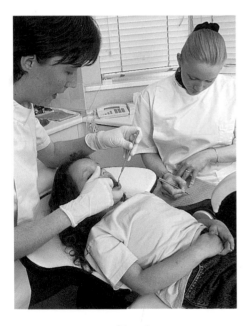

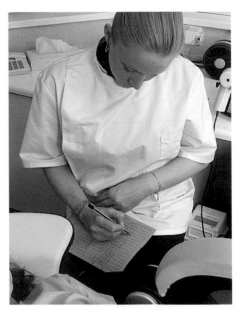

2 Katrina tells Marie which of Hannah's teeth have grown.

3 Marie marks them on Hannah's dental record card.

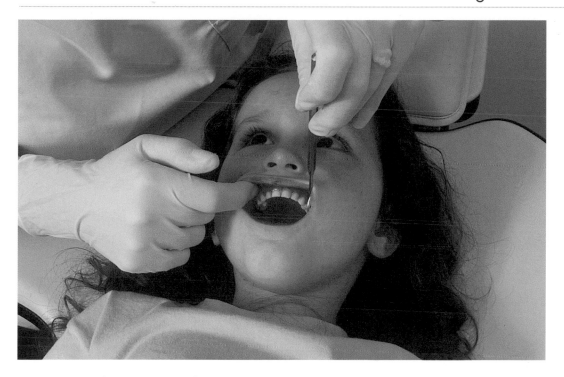

4 Katrina has another good look.

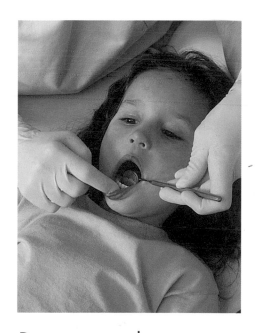

5 Bottom teeth…

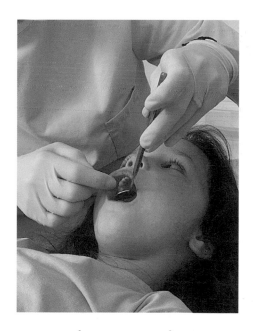

6 …and top teeth.

Can you see the back of Hannah's teeth in the mirrored tool?

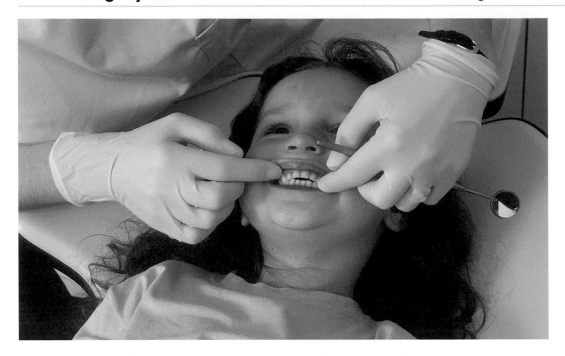

1 Katrina asks Hannah to bite her teeth together. This shows how Hannah's teeth line up.

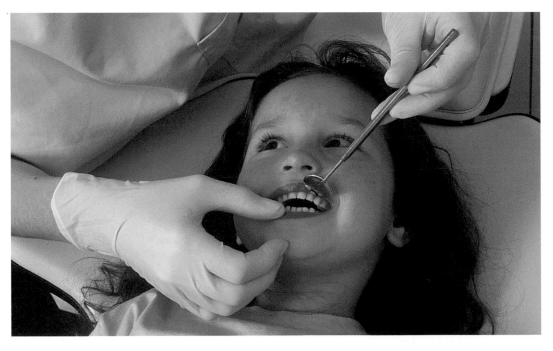

2 Hannah sometimes sucks her thumb. When her second teeth come through, her thumb may begin to push her front teeth forward. Katrina will watch for this.

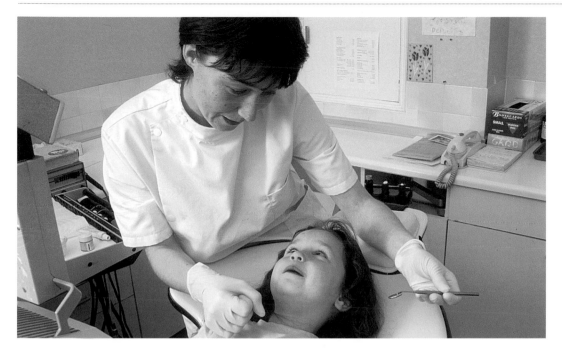

3 Katrina is very pleased with Hannah's teeth. She reminds Hannah to brush her teeth for 2-3 minutes each day after breakfast and before she goes to bed.

4 Katrina has now finished looking at Hannah's teeth. She takes off her rubber gloves.

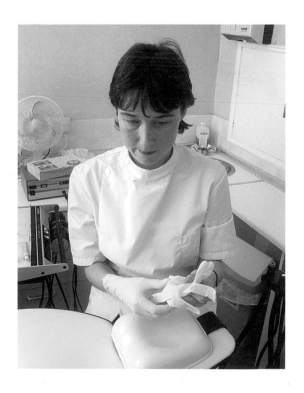

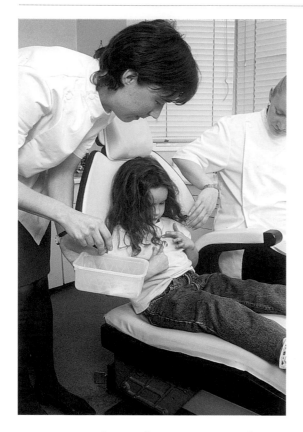

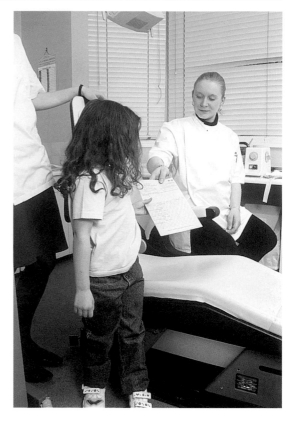

1 Katrina has let Hannah choose a sticker for having her teeth looked at today.
Hannah has chosen one with a rainbow.

2 Marie gives Hannah her special record card to give to Jackie, the receptionist.

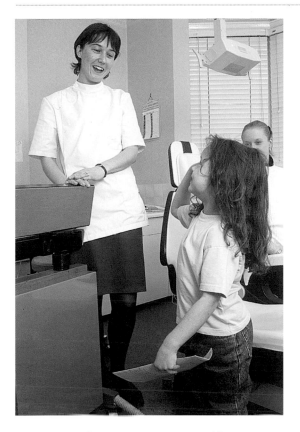

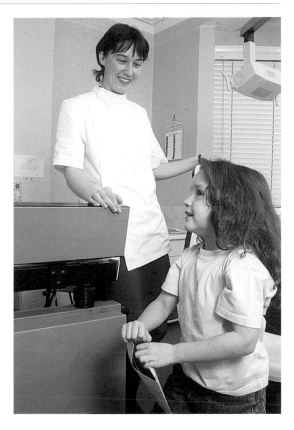

3 Hannah says goodbye to Katrina and Marie.

4 She goes back to the waiting room.

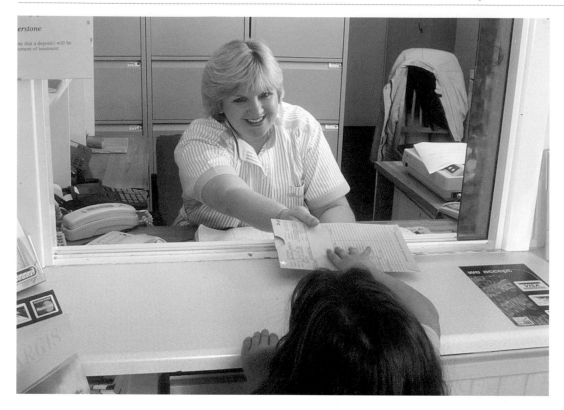

1 Hannah gives her special record card to Jackie.

2 Jackie asks mummy to sign her name to say Hannah has visited the dentist today.

Hannah waves goodbye to Jackie.
When Hannah comes next time to the see Katrina, the dentist, she may not be so shy.

Katrina says, 'it is very important to look after your teeth and keep them strong and healthy.'

Let us look at how to clean teeth.

1 Place your toothbrush at the edge of the gums and brush gently with a circular motion. Don't forget always to brush the top *and* bottom teeth.

2 Brush all around the outside.

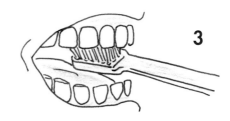

3 Brush all around the inside.

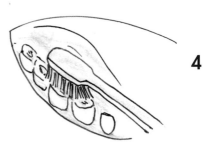

4 Brush all the biting surfaces backwards and forwards.

• Always let mummy or daddy check your teeth after you have cleaned them to make sure you haven't missed any areas of your teeth.

Before you go to bed tonight will you practise cleaning your teeth like Katrina says?

Katrina says, 'teeth are really interesting. Without them we would not be able to bite, or chew our food.'

Let us look at milk teeth, which are also called 'first teeth' or 'baby teeth'.

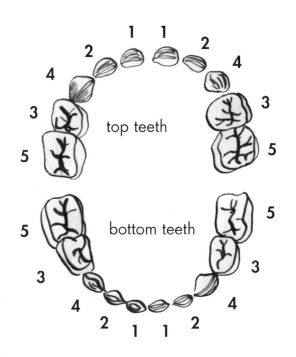

top teeth

bottom teeth

There are 20 milk teeth. Here is a guide to when they come through the gums and what they are called.

1 Incisors appear at 6–12 months.
2 Incisors appear at 9–16 months.
3 Molars appear at 12–18 months.
4 Canines appear at 18 months – 2 years.
5 Molars appear at 2–3 years

When the milk teeth come out they are replaced with permanent teeth, which are also called 'second teeth'.

Katrina says, 'let us look at the inside of a tooth.'

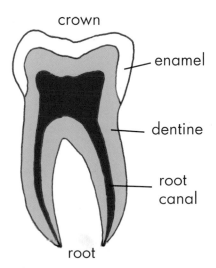

crown

enamel

dentine

root canal

root

Katrina says, 'try using a disclosing tablet to see if you are brushing your teeth correctly.'

Hannah is going to use one. Let us see what happened.

Katrina's tip: 'If you do not want coloured lips, put Vaseline on them first.'

1

Hannah has eaten lots of different foods today but her teeth look OK.

2

She puts the red disclosing tablet in her mouth to chew it up.

3

The tablet mixes with her saliva. Hannah is not sure she likes the taste!

4

She has a sip of water to rinse out her mouth.

5

Now Hannah spits out the water.

6

Look at her teeth – can you see how red they are?

7

The red shows the plaque – a build-up of bacteria on the teeth.

8

Plaque must be removed by careful brushing.

9

Hannah is using a mirror so that she can see how she is doing.

10

She brushes the front teeth with a circular motion.

11

Look how red Hannah's tongue is! She thinks this is funny!

12

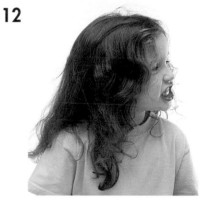

She checks with mummy.

13

There is a little more left to clean.

14

Hannah has a final check in the mirror and …

15

…Yes! Hannah has lovely clean teeth.

Can you name everyone on these pages?

Bye bye ... !

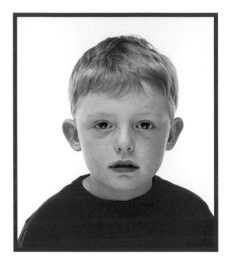

Bye bye ... !

Bye bye ... ,
and ... !

Bye bye ... !

Bye bye … !

Bye bye … !

Now it is time to say bye bye to
Hannah, Anthony, Kathy and Jessica;
Jackie the receptionist,
Marie the dental nurse,
and of course Katrina the dentist.
Bye bye!

Your baby's teeth

Keeping your baby's mouth healthy from birth and giving a good diet will help develop good teeth and lessen dental problems later. So never put sugary drinks in your baby's feeding bottles for her to suck on.

Teething can be an uncomfortable time for both you and your baby, affecting her eyes, ears, nose and throat. Try using teething gels or sugar-free paracetamol to ease her discomfort. You can start brushing your baby's first tooth as soon as you see it appearing above the gum. Some babies are born with a tooth and this also needs brushing.

Brushing teeth

There are many ways to introduce your baby to cleaning teeth. One way is to sit her on your knee so you can see inside her mouth. Place a pea-sized blob of toothpaste on a baby toothbrush and gently brush each tooth in a circular motion. Most babies and children love the taste of toothpaste and will eat most of it! You can buy baby and junior brushes which have rounded ends as well as mild toothpastes containing fluoride. Make brushing teeth a fun part of the morning and night-time routine.

Brushing conflicts

Some children refuse to open their mouths and dislike the feeling of brushing. Early conflicts and frustration can develop into a battleground at the beginning and at the end of the day, when you least need it. Teeth have to be brushed, so introducing your child to the routine early will be easier, and turning it into a fun time together will get better results. Try the following:

- Your child loves to copy you. Let her watch you clean your teeth. Let her be 'mummy' and clean *your* teeth.
- Make different noises and mouth shapes together to encourage her to open her mouth.
- Playing 'brush your teeth in the bath' is great fun: frothing, blowing bubbles, gargling and so on.
- Sing a song, 'this is the way we brush our teeth…'
- Use a mirror to show and talk to her about her teeth.
- Praise any steps forward, however small.

Visiting the dentist

If your child has not yet visited a dentist, don't worry: dentists are used to helping children get familiar with what happens. Try not to wait until your child has something wrong with her teeth before the first visit. The combination of pain and a new experience could leave your child with a fear of the dentist that can last a lifetime. Children can find unfamilar surroundings, bright lights, a strange person wanting to put fingers and a metal object inside their mouth very frightening. Refusing to open their mouth is common, as is being cooperative one visit and not the next. You can help your child by being supportive and working with the dentist.

Phobias

If you have had a bad experience at the dentist, try not to mention it to your child. If she thinks it was unpleasant for you, she will imagine it will be horrific for her. It is worth remembering that technology and treatments are improving all the time.

Sweet things and teeth

We all like sweet things, but sugar encourages tooth decay. Adverts and relentless demands make it difficult not to use sweets as bribes, comforters or distractions. Try to help by giving a low sugar diet, use sugar-free medicine and do not give sugary drinks before bed. Snack foods like twiglets, cheesestrings and breadsticks are better. Fruit and sliced raw vegetables are best. When giving a 'treat', choose a chocolate bar, which is better than boiled sweets that are sucked for a long time. Offer sweet treats after a meal, not before.

If your child has an accident and damages a tooth

Loss of first teeth or discolouration is not unusual.

If your child has a tooth knocked out, replace the tooth in its socket or store the tooth in your own mouth (saliva) or in milk and immediately visit the dentist. Speed is crucial, so visit the dentist immediately and she will give the best treatment to try to save the tooth. The loss of a tooth can be either exciting or scary. Tooth fairies can be very useful in helping overcome this problem!

First published in 2000 by CP Publishing
Richmond, Surrey, United Kingdom

Text Copyright © 1998 Helen & Clive Dorman
Photographs Copyright © 1998 Helen Dorman
This edition Copyright © 2000 The Children's Project Ltd

Illustrations by Nicky Plumbley

Helen and Clive Dorman have asserted their moral right to be identified as the authors of this work in accordance with the Copyright, Design and Patents Act 1988.

ISBN 1 903275 03 2

Printed in Hong Kong

Acknowledgements

We would like to thank Ham Dental Surgery, Richmond for their cooperation. Special thanks to Katrina McLaren, Marie Bailey, Jackie Wheeler, Kathy, Anthony and Jessica Blair and, of course, Hannah.